AR PTS: 0.5

Searchlight
BOOKS™

What Do You
Know about
Maps?

Using

Physical Maps

Rebecca E. Hirsch

Lerner Publications ◆ Minneapolis

Lerner Publications Company
A division of Lerner Publishing Group, Inc.
241 First Avenue North
Minneapolis, MN 55401 USA

For reading levels and more information, look up this title at www.lernerbooks.com.

Library of Congress Cataloging-in-Publication Data

Names: Hirsch, Rebecca E., author.
Title: Using physical maps / by Rebecca E. Hirsch.
Description: Minneapolis : Lerner Publications, [2017] | Series: Searchlight books. What do you know about maps? | Includes bibliographical references and index. | Audience: Age 8–11. | Audience: Grades 4–6.
Identifiers: LCCN 2015038367| ISBN 9781512409499 (lb : alk. paper) | ISBN 9781512412932 (pb : alk. paper) | ISBN 9781512410730 (eb pdf)
Subjects: LCSH: Map reading—Juvenile literature. | Topographic maps—Juvenile literature.
Classification: LCC GA130 .H558 2017 | DDC 912.01/4—dc23

LC record available at http://lccn.loc.gov/2015038367

Manufactured in the United States of America
1-39538-21242-2/24/2016

Contents

Chapter 1

WHAT IS A PHYSICAL MAP?

Maps are like a gateway to the world! They can help you find almost any place on Earth. Maps are diagrams that show us places. They use symbols to show the features of a place. Maps show us different things. A park map might show where to find trees and a playground. A city map may show streets, a public pool, and a science museum.

PHILADELPHIA

To Valley Forge National Historic Park, Pennsylvania Dutch Country & Pocono Mountains

Girard College
S College Ave
Girard Ave
Ridge Ave
Fairmount Ave
N 6th St
N 5th St
Fairmount Ave
Schuylkill Expressway
Philadelphia Museum of Art
Eakins Oval
Spring Garden St
Spring Garden St
Ridge Ave
Edgar Allan Poe National Historic Site
Powelton St
Vine St Expressway
Franklin Institute Science Museum
30th St Amtrack Station
Logan Circle & Square
John F Kennedy Blvd
Market St
China
Market St
Chestnut St
University City
University of Pennsylvania
Rittenhouse Square
Rosenbach Museum & Library
Civil War Library & Museum
Broad St
Perry Ave
South St
South
Societ Hill
Sculpture Garden

0 ——— 0.5 km
0 ——— 0.3 mile

Maps show where to find things like libraries and museums. Which place looks most interesting to you on this map?

Maps serve many purposes. Some maps show country boundaries and locations of states. Others focus on which areas produce different crops. Still others call out natural features. They use colors to show mountains, valleys, lakes, and rivers. These maps also show the location of these features and the distances between them. Maps that show natural features are called physical maps.

This physical map of the world uses blue to show water, brown to show deserts, and green to show vegetation (trees and other growing things).

A Bird's-Eye View

Physical maps show us a view of the world from above. When you walk through a park, you see the world from your own viewpoint. You might see a stream beside you and some trees ahead of you. If you lie down on the ground and look up, the world looks different. You might see clouds overhead and a bird flying.

Physical maps are a little like photos taken from above. They show things as they'd look if you saw them from the sky.

Imagine what the bird sees as it flies high over the park. From high in the sky, it looks down on the world. We call this a bird's-eye view. Physical maps give a bird's-eye, or aerial, view of the world. When you look at a physical map, you are looking at a place from above, much as a bird might see it.

This aerial view shows crisscrossing roads.

Why Physical Maps Are Useful

No single map can show everything about a place. Before making a map, cartographers, or mapmakers, must decide on the purpose of the map and how people will use it. They must decide what place they want to show. They must choose what features will be useful to people using the map.

WHAT FEATURES MIGHT A CARTOGRAPHER PUT ON A MAP OF HIKING TRAILS?

A physical map may show country boundaries and where states or provinces are. But its main purpose isn't to show human-made places like states and countries. It's to show natural features. A physical map may also show the elevation of the land, meaning its height above sea level, and specific types of vegetation, such as forests or grasslands.

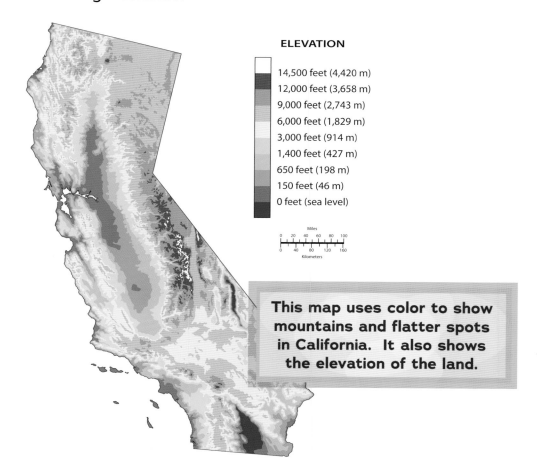

ELEVATION

14,500 feet (4,420 m)
12,000 feet (3,658 m)
9,000 feet (2,743 m)
6,000 feet (1,829 m)
3,000 feet (914 m)
1,400 feet (427 m)
650 feet (198 m)
150 feet (46 m)
0 feet (sea level)

Miles
0   20   40   60   80   100
0   40   80   120   160
Kilometers

This map uses color to show mountains and flatter spots in California. It also shows the elevation of the land.

A physical map is useful. If you live in a place with mountains, you can find the names and locations of those mountains. You can use a physical map to explore a place and find your way. If you are studying a state or a country, a physical map can help you understand the features of that place.

Many different people find physical maps helpful. A road builder might use a physical map to figure out the best route for a new road. A city planner might use one to find a good place to build a school. Someone on a camping trip could look to a physical map to find a river where she could go fishing.

A lot of planning goes into building things. Maps are one tool builders use in their planning.

Did You Know?

More than a hundred years ago, a scientist named Alfred Wegener noticed something on world maps. Some of the continents, such as South America and Africa, fit together like puzzle pieces. Mountain ranges in South America seemed to fit together with mountain ranges in Africa. Wegener guessed that the continents had been joined long ago in one huge landmass. Modern scientists call this ancient landmass Pangaea. That is Greek for "all lands."

This globe shows how the continents may have looked when they were joined.

Chapter 2

WHAT'S ON A PHYSICAL MAP?

Physical maps are drawn smaller than the places they represent. Everything on the map is drawn to scale. This means that every object is in the same place as the real thing, but the size is smaller.

The mountains on this map of Switzerland are much bigger in real life than they are on the map! What is it called when things on a map are drawn at a smaller size?

The area shown on a physical map determines the map's scale. Large-scale maps show small areas, such as a park. Large-scale maps show a lot of detail. Since the scale is large, natural features appear large on the map.

The mountains on this map graphic of a park look much larger than they do on the map of Switzerland.

Small-scale maps show big areas, such as a country, a continent, or even the whole world. Since the area shown is large, not a lot of detail is shown on a small-scale map. Natural features on the map appear small.

Compare this map to the map graphic on page 13. This map doesn't show any ponds, as the park map does. There are ponds in the United States, of course. But you can't see them on this map.

Physical maps are available on computers. These maps allow you to zoom in and out, which changes the scale of the map. At first, you may look at a physical map of an entire country. As you zoom in, you may look at just an area of the country with a lot of mountains. As you zoom in farther, you may look at just one mountain.

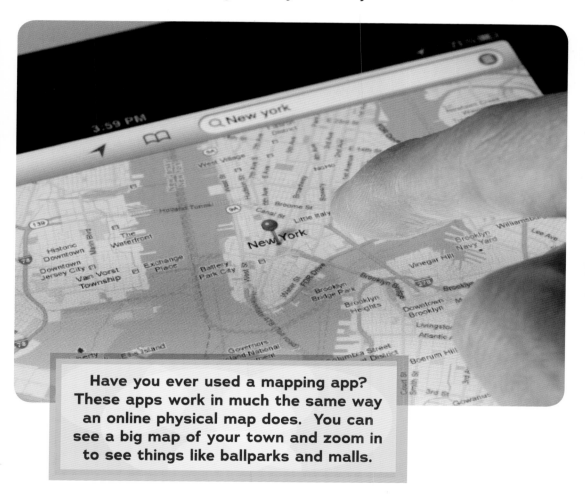

Have you ever used a mapping app? These apps work in much the same way an online physical map does. You can see a big map of your town and zoom in to see things like ballparks and malls.

Maps Then and Now

People invented maps thousands of years ago. Ancient people carved maps on rocks or clay. In later times, people made maps using brushes and parchment. Modern mapmakers draw maps using computers with special software.

Modern mapmaking relies a great deal on technology.

Symbols, Colors, and More

Physical maps often use symbols in addition to colors. The symbols help to show what different features are. For example, a map may use green to show vegetation. On top of the green, you may see tree symbols that tell you the vegetation is in a forest.

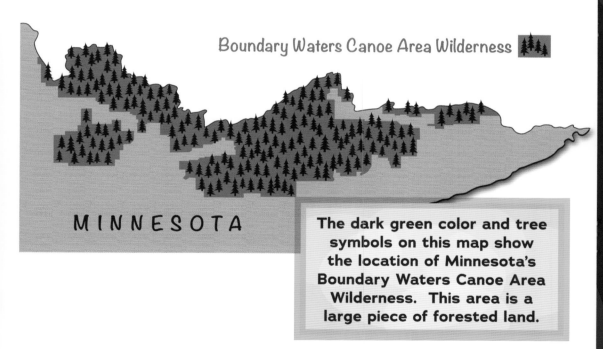

Boundary Waters Canoe Area Wilderness

MINNESOTA

The dark green color and tree symbols on this map show the location of Minnesota's Boundary Waters Canoe Area Wilderness. This area is a large piece of forested land.

Physical maps often use color to show elevation in addition to natural features. Higher elevations may be shown in darker colors. Lower spots may appear in lighter colors.

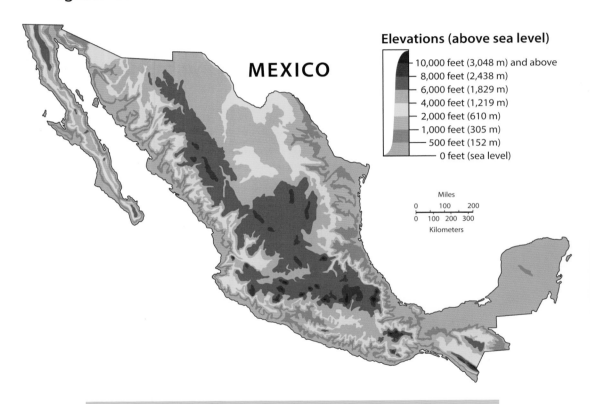

MEXICO

Elevations (above sea level)

- 10,000 feet (3,048 m) and above
- 8,000 feet (2,438 m)
- 6,000 feet (1,829 m)
- 4,000 feet (1,219 m)
- 2,000 feet (610 m)
- 1,000 feet (305 m)
- 500 feet (152 m)
- 0 feet (sea level)

Miles
0   100   200
0   100   200   300
Kilometers

This map of Mexico uses dark brown to show high mountains and light green to show valleys.

YELLOWSTONE NATIONAL PARK

MONTANA

WYOMING

IDAHO

Absaroka-Beartooth Wilderness

Gardiner

Cooke City

Mammoth Hot Springs

Lamar Valley

Tower-Roosevelt

Hebgen Lake

YELLOWSTONE NATIONAL PARK

West Yellowstone

Canyon Village

Norris Geyser Basin

Lake Village

Old Faithful

Yellowstone Lake

Wapiti Valley

Caribou-Targhee National Forest

Grant Village

Heart Lake

Shoshone National Forest

Yellowstone River

National forests
State border
Highway
Town/village
Geothermal site

This map of Yellowstone National Park uses colors, labels, and symbols to show both natural and human-made features.

Physical maps do sometimes include features made by people. A physical map of a national park, for instance, may show the location of hiking trails, roads, and nearby cities or states. Some physical maps show the location of state or country capitals.

Other Helpful Features

Physical maps have other features that help you use them. The title of a map tells you what the map is about. It might tell you the type of map and what part of the world the map shows.

Many physical maps have a tool called a compass rose. It looks like a compass. It shows you which way on the map is north, east, south, and west.

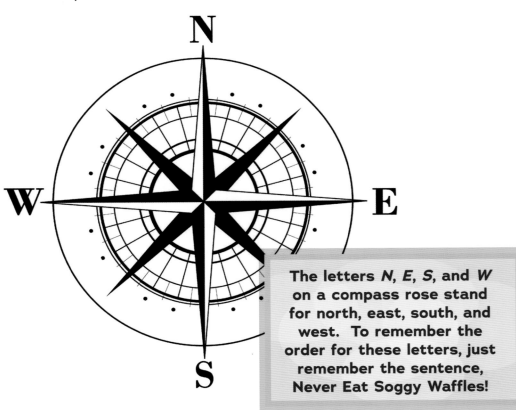

The letters *N*, *E*, *S*, and *W* on a compass rose stand for north, east, south, and west. To remember the order for these letters, just remember the sentence, **Never Eat Soggy Waffles!**

Some physical maps have a grid with lines running up and down and side to side. The lines that run up and down show north and south. The lines that run side to side show east and west.

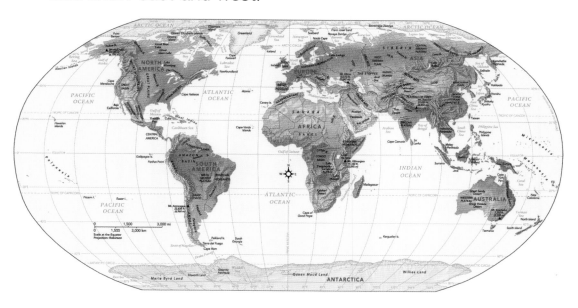

YOUR CLASSROOM MAY HAVE A MAP ON THE WALL THAT INCLUDES LINES LIKE THE ONES ON THIS MAP.

The north-south lines on a map are called longitude lines. The east-west lines are latitude lines. The latitude line in the middle of Earth is the equator. It splits the world into a northern half and a southern half. What countries does the equator pass through on this physical map of South America?

Latitude and longitude lines are not real lines on the ground. They are invisible lines that exist only on maps.

Did You Know?

A physical map is flat, like a sheet of paper. But Earth is not flat. If you look at a globe, you can see that Earth is round. A globe shows the true shape of Earth. Cartographers have to transfer information from the round Earth to make a flat map. They must squeeze and stretch different parts of the world to make everything flat. This transfer of information is called projection. Because of projection, Greenland, for example, often appears much larger on maps than it is in real life.

Greenland doesn't look much smaller than Canada on this map. But Canada's land area is more than 3 million square miles (7.8 million square kilometers), while Greenland's is only about 158,000 square miles (409,218 sq. km).

Chapter 3

HOW DO YOU USE A PHYSICAL MAP?

Using a physical map means knowing how to use its tools and read its symbols. The scale tool helps you understand distances on the map. It shows that a certain distance on the map stands for a certain distance on Earth.

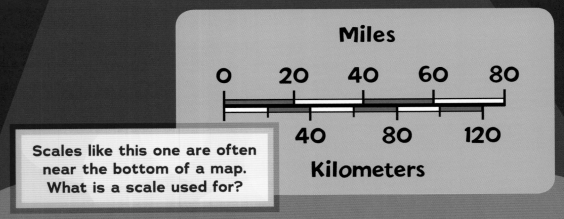

Miles

0   20   40   60   80

40   80   120

Kilometers

Scales like this one are often near the bottom of a map. What is a scale used for?

Maps have different types of scales. One common type looks like a ruler. Scales like this are often marked with miles, kilometers, or both. To use this kind of scale, line up the edge of a sheet of paper between two locations on a map. Make a mark on the paper at each spot. Then move the paper to the scale. Line up one mark with the zero. The other mark will be on or near a number that shows the distance.

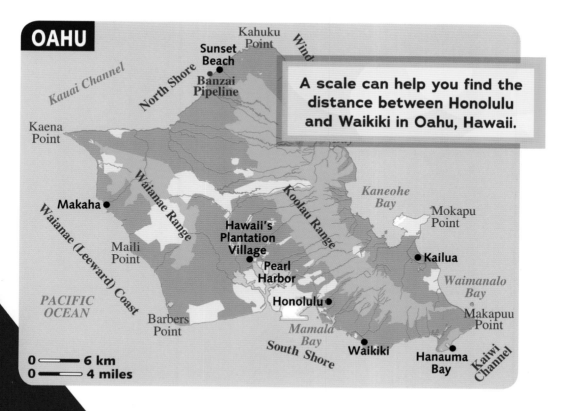

A scale can help you find the distance between Honolulu and Waikiki in Oahu, Hawaii.

Another type of scale gives information in words. For example, it might say, "1 inch (2.5 centimeters) = 1,000 miles (1,609 kilometers)." This means that 1 inch on the map equals 1,000 miles on the ground. To use this kind of scale, measure the distance between two points with a ruler. Multiply the inches by 1,000, and you'll have the actual distance in miles.

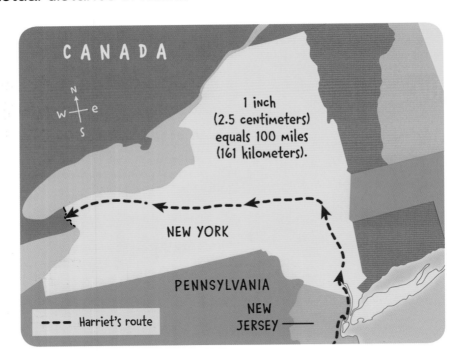

TO USE SCALES GIVEN IN WORDS, YOU'LL NEED TO DO A LITTLE MATH.

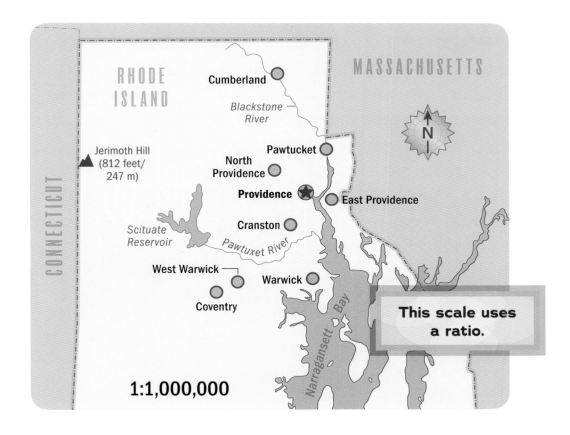

RHODE ISLAND

MASSACHUSETTS

Cumberland

Blackstone River

N

Jerimoth Hill
(812 feet/
247 m)

Pawtucket

North Providence

Providence

East Providence

Scituate Reservoir

Cranston

Pawtuxet River

West Warwick

Warwick

Coventry

CONNECTICUT

Narragansett Bay

This scale uses a ratio.

1:1,000,000

Still other scales use fractions or ratios. They might look like this: 1/1,000,000 (a fraction) or 1:1,000,000 (a ratio). In these examples, the scale is telling you that the map is one million times smaller than the place in real life. So 1 inch (2.5 cm) on the map represents 1,000,000 inches (2,500,000 cm) on Earth, or almost 16 miles (26 km).

Legends, Symbols, and Colors

A legend is the key to understanding the symbols on a map. A legend is usually a box on a map that shows different symbols and tells you what they stand for. For example, a legend might include a triangle symbol and tell you that it stands for a mountain.

Legends can also include colors. They might tell you that a map uses red to show areas that have an elevation of 12,000 feet (3,658 meters). Or it might tell you that it uses green for areas lower than 500 feet (152 m).

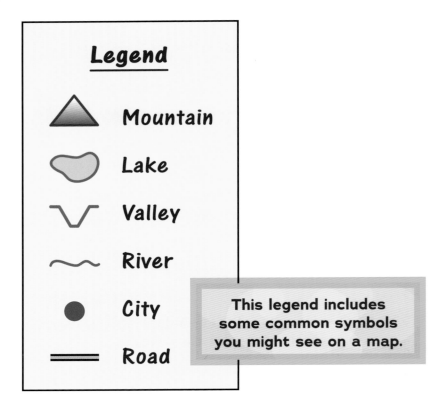

This legend includes some common symbols you might see on a map.

Mapping the Ocean

Scientists have mapped the ocean floor using sound waves. They bounce sound waves off the ocean floor. The echo tells them how deep it is. Sound waves show that the ocean floor has tall mountains, deep canyons, and wide plains.

There's much more than meets the eye underneath the ocean's waves! Sound-wave mapping has shown that the ocean's landscape is just as varied as the landscapes we see above water.

Using the Grid

The grid made up of latitude and longitude lines can help you find places on a map. Latitude and longitude lines cross one another at places called coordinates. The coordinates are like a global address. Every place on Earth is at a certain coordinate.

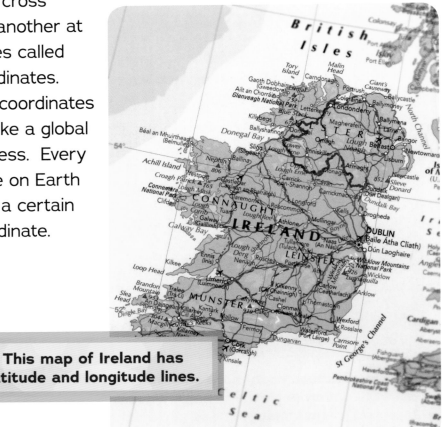

This map of Ireland has latitude and longitude lines.

To use latitude and longitude lines to find a place on a physical map, simply look up the latitude and longitude of the place. You can do this through a web search. A librarian can also help you find a resource that has this information.

Latitude and longitude are measured in degrees. The measurements also have a letter after them that stands for one of the four directions: north, east, south, or west. The latitude and longitude of Buffalo, New York, for example, is 42 degrees north and 78 degrees west. Once you know a place's latitude and longitude, find the lines that mark that latitude and longitude on a map. Follow the lines to the spot where they meet. You've found your place!

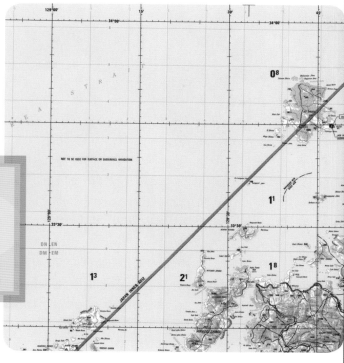

Latitude and longitude lines are labeled on the sides, top, and bottom of most maps. Look there for the measurements of the place you want to find.

Grids and Large-Scale Maps

The grids on some large-scale maps have numbers and letters instead of latitude or longitude measurements. For example, a pond may be at C2. You find things on these maps the same way that you do on maps with latitude and longitude lines. First, find column C. The label for this column will be across the top of the map. Then find row 2. Its label will be along the side. The pond is where column C and row 2 meet.

With just a little know-how, you'll soon be reading maps like a pro!

Chapter 4

ARE YOU A PHYSICAL MAP WHIZ?

By now, you know a lot about physical maps. It's time to put that knowledge to the test! But don't worry. This test will be quick and fun. It will even let you go on a virtual vacation!

Take a look at this physical map of the United States. Which states have the features you'd most like to see?

Washington, Oregon, Montana, North Dakota, Minnesota, Wisconsin, Michigan, Maine, Vermont, New York, New Hampshire, Massachusetts, Idaho, Wyoming, South Dakota, Iowa, Illinois, Indiana, Ohio, West Virginia, Pennsylvania, Rhode Island, Connecticut, New Jersey, Delaware, Washington, DC, Maryland, Virginia, Nevada, Utah, Colorado, Nebraska, Kansas, Missouri, Kentucky, North Carolina, South Carolina, California, Arizona, New Mexico, Oklahoma, Tennessee, Arkansas, Georgia, Texas, Louisiana, Mississippi, Alabama, Florida, Alaska, Hawaii

Mountains
Plains
Deciduous forest
Desert
Coniferous forest
Lake
Tropical rain forest

To get started, imagine that you live in Virginia. Your family is taking a vacation to the mountains in your state. You live in an area of the state known as the coastal plains. Look at the map. What color represents the area where you live? What mountain range will you be visiting?

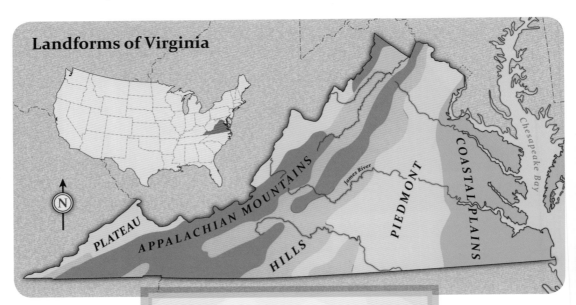

Landforms of Virginia

N

PLATEAU

APPALACHIAN MOUNTAINS

James River

HILLS

PIEDMONT

COASTAL PLAINS

Chesapeake Bay

In addition to the coastal plains and Appalachian Mountains, what other areas do you see on this map of Virginia?

As your family is driving through the mountains, you decide to camp for the night. You find a campsite next to a river. Your dad tells you that this same river flows near the town where you live, in the coastal plains. Look at the map on page 34. What river do you think he is talking about? What body of water does it flow into?

RIVERS OFTEN FLOW THROUGH MANY DIFFERENT AREAS—AND SOMETIMES EVEN THROUGH DIFFERENT STATES.

Maps can tell you a lot about places both near and far!

You Did It!

Congratulations! You've learned how to use a physical map. These maps help you learn about the natural features of places. They can even help you find your way. They show features such as mountains, forests, lakes, and rivers. Physical maps are a great way to explore your world.

Fun Facts

- Physical maps not only show the height of mountains. They also show depressions, or areas of land that lie below sea level. The lowest point on Earth is the shore of the Dead Sea, near Israel. It lies about 1,360 feet (415 m) below sea level.

- The deepest part of the ocean is known as the Mariana Trench. It is in the Pacific Ocean. The trench is more than 36,201 feet (11,033 m) deep. That's nearly 7 miles (11 km) down!

- Some cartographers don't map Earth. Instead, they use images taken from space to create physical maps of the moon and Mars. Martian maps show valleys, craters, and dry riverbeds.

Glossary

aerial: high up in the air

cartographer: a person who makes maps

compass rose: a circle showing directions

coordinate: a set of numbers used to locate a point on a map

elevation: the height above sea level

grid: a network of horizontal and vertical lines at right angles, used for locating points on a map

latitude: a distance north or south of the equator measured in degrees

legend: an explanatory list of symbols on a map

longitude: a distance east or west of the prime meridian measured in degrees

projection: a method of showing the curved surface of Earth on a flat map

ratio: the quotient of two numbers. The ratio of 1 to 100 may be expressed as 1:100 or 1/100.

scale: a tool that explains the size of a map compared to the actual place it represents

vegetation: plant life

Learn More about Physical Maps

Books

Brown, Cynthia Light, and Patrick M. McGinty. *Mapping and Navigation: Explore the History and Science of Finding Your Way with 20 Projects*. White River Junction, VT: Nomad, 2013. Explore the world of maps and mapmaking with hands-on projects and interesting facts.

Petersen, Christine. *Learning about North America*. Minneapolis: Lerner Publications, 2016. Find out more about North America's landforms as well as other features such as climate, countries, and cultures.

Rajczak, Kristen. *Latitude and Longitude*. New York: Gareth Stevens, 2015. Check out this book to learn more about latitude and longitude.

Websites

CIA: *The World Factbook*
https://www.cia.gov/library/publications/resources/the-world-factbook
Look up regional and world maps, as well as facts about any country in the world, in *The World Factbook* on the US Central Intelligence Agency's website.

Kids.gov: Social Studies
https://kids.usa.gov/social-studies/index.shtml
Learn more about the world with photos, facts, and maps you can print.

National Geographic: Atlas Explorer
http://ngm.nationalgeographic.com/map/atlas
Zoom in on physical maps of Africa, Antarctica, Asia, Australia, Europe, North America, South America, and the oceans of the world.

Index

Photo Acknowledgments

The images in this book are used with the permission of: © Lonely Planet/Getty Images, p. 4; © Nordic Photos/SuperStock, p. 5; © iStockphoto.com/bjones27, p. 6; © Michael H/Stone/Getty Images, p. 7; © iStockphoto.com/Christopher Futcher, pp. 8, 16; © Laura Westlund/Independent Picture Service, pp. 9, 17, 18, 19, 24, 26, 27, 28, 33, 34; © Erik Isakson/Blend Images/SuperStock, p. 10; © Russ Widstrand/Photolibrary/Getty Images, p. 11; © Planet Observer/Universal Images Group/Getty Images, p. 12; © Michael Schmeling/Alamy, p. 14; © iStockphoto.com/ymgerman, p. 15; © Makhnach/Dreamstime.com, p. 20; © Globe Turner, LLC/Getty Images, p. 21; © NG MAPS/ National Geographic Creative, p. 22; © delpieroo/Deposit Photos, p. 23; © Lonely Planet/Getty Images, p. 25; © iStockphoto.com/shannonstent, p. 29; © iStockphoto.com/omersukrugoksu, p. 30; US Geological Survey, p. 31; © Corbis/SuperStock, p. 32; © iStockphoto.com/frwooar, p. 35; © iStockphoto.com/Neonci, p. 36.

Front cover: © Laura Westlund/Independent Picture Service (map); © iStockphoto.com/Devaev Dmitriy (background).

Main body text set in Adrianna Regular 14/20.
Typeface provided by Chank.